I AM BEYOND

Limitation

Angela Gadiare

 **I AM BEYOND LIMITATION**

Royal Diadem Publishing

Copyright © 2025 Angela Gadiare

All rights reserved. No part of this book may be reproduced, distributed, or transmitted in any form by any means, graphics, electronics, or mechanical, including photocopy, recording, taping, or by any means or stored in a database or retrieval system, without the prior written permission of the publisher except in the case of reprints in the context of reviews, quotes, or references.

All bible scriptures references are taken from the Holy Writings in English Standard, New King James Version, King James Version, New International Version, New American Standard Version, Amplified Bible, and the Living Bible. Used by permission. All rights reserved.

Printed in the United States of America
First Edition: November 2025

"Arise, shine, for your light has come, and the glory of the LORD rises upon you."
— Isaiah 60:1 (NIV)

Dedication

To the God who writes beauty through broken places—this book is for You. Every page is a thank-You note, every paragraph a hallelujah.

To the brave ones who refuse to let limitations have the last word—may you hear your courage calling and answer with a resounding yes.

To my children and all the sons and daughters watching us learn, try, fall, and rise—may our everyday faith become your favorite inheritance.

To the ancestors and trailblazers who prayed us forward, sowed in tears, and believed before the evidence—your whispers still lift our wings.

To the readers who carry this message into kitchens, classrooms, boardrooms, and quiet midnight battles—may these words meet you like fresh wind and holy fire.

And to the next generation, known and unknown—take our small seeds and walk boldly. Love loudly. Live like grace is true.

Table of Contents

Dedication 6
Acknowledgment 10
Introduction 12
Declaration 15
The Power of Faith In The Face of Limitation .. 16
Embracing Your Struggles as Catalysts for Growth 23
Trusting In God's Timing 30
Overcoming Self-Doubt and Embracing Your True Identity 37
The Importance of Serving Beyond Yourself ... 46
Navigating the Valley of the Shadow of Death 53
Walking Boldly In The Call of God 62
Living A Life Beyond Limitations 69
Leaving A Legacy of Faith 78
A New Beginning Beyond Limitation 85
Personal Legacy 92
CONCLUSION: The Echo You Leave 97
JOURNAL SECTION 99
A Final Blessing 145

Acknowledgment

It is with a grateful heart that I acknowledge the goodness and mercy of God in my life. Looking back on my journey, I am overwhelmed with gratitude for how far God has brought me. Truly, all honor, praise, and glory belong to Him, who is the author and finisher of my faith.

As I reflect on my journey, I am reminded of the people who have been instrumental in my life, and who have helped me along the way. To my son, Shevone Robinson, you are my world. Your unwavering love and support have been a source of strength for me during some of the toughest moments of my life. God used you to remind me of His love and faithfulness.

I am also grateful for the spiritual parents that God has placed in my life. To Pastor Esther Brand, who I affectionately call mom, thank you for being a mother figure to me when I needed it the most. Your love, guidance, and prayers have been a blessing in my life. To Mr. Joseph Brand, who I call dad, thank you for your support and guidance. I am blessed to have you both in my life. Pastor Jeffery Mayers thank you for all the prayers and support. Minister Michael Learmond, I appreciate all your prayers. Deaconess Mayers I thank you for your hugs when I really needed them. Missionary Merl Smith and Brother Milton Smith I thank you for always being there for me.

I am also grateful for my siblings, Diana Gadiare, Joy Gadiare, Donna Gadiare, Ray Gadiare, Glenton Gadiare, Robert Gadiare, and Audrey Gadiare. Your love and support have been a constant source of strength for me. I also want to express my gratitude to all my friends and family. I thank you for your prayers and kind words.

Introduction

Life has a way of throwing us into storms we never saw coming. Sometimes it's illness, heartbreak, or financial struggle. Other times, it's something so unexpected, it takes our breath away. For me, it was my voice — one of the most basic, yet essential, parts of who I was.

One morning, without warning, my voice was gone. No gradual decline. No clear explanation. One day, I could speak, laugh, and share my heart freely. The next day, silence. Doctors didn't have answers, specialists couldn't fix it, and I was left facing an unsettling reality: a life without the very tool I had always used to express myself.

At first, the silence was suffocating. I felt isolated, helpless, and even questioned my purpose. How could I contribute to the world if I couldn't speak? How could I inspire, encourage, or simply connect without a voice? It felt like more than just a physical loss — it was emotional, mental, and deeply spiritual.

But here's the truth: what felt like the end was really the beginning. That silence became sacred. In it, I discovered strength I didn't know I had, and I found myself leaning more fully on God. I realized my voice was never just sound — it was my spirit, my heart, my faith, and my presence in the world. Losing it taught me that communication is not only about words, but about how we live, love, and show up even when life feels broken.

Through prayer, reflection, and perseverance, I began to see my limitations differently. What once looked like a barrier became a doorway to growth. I learned that with faith, even our deepest struggles can become stepping stones. God was showing me that my story wasn't over — it was being rewritten.

This book, *I Am Beyond Limitation*, isn't just my testimony. It's a message for anyone who feels trapped by what they cannot do, cannot see, or cannot change. Maybe your limitation is physical. Maybe it's emotional pain, financial hardship, or mental battles that no one else can see. Whatever form it takes, I want you to know this: your limitations are not the end of your story. They might be the very thing that unlocks the greater version of who you were always meant to be.

Faith is the foundation of a limitless life. Faith is what reminds us that even in the silence, God is speaking. It is faith that strengthens us to rise when the world tells us to sit down. It is faith that declares, "I am not defined by my struggles — I am defined by God's purpose for my life."

Alongside faith, I discovered the power of mindset. Our thoughts shape our reality. If we believe we are stuck, we will live stuck. But if we believe that with God's help we can rise above, we start to live differently. A limitless mindset doesn't deny pain or pretend challenges don't exist. It simply refuses to let those challenges define the outcome.

In these pages, I'll share the lessons I've learned, the mindset shifts that carried me forward, and the spiritual truths that continue to guide me. My hope is that as you read, you'll begin to see yourself differently. That you'll recognize the power already inside you, planted by God, waiting to be activated.

You are not your past. You are not your pain. You are not your limitations. You are a child of God, created with intention, destined with purpose, and fully capable of living a life without limits.

So, let's begin this journey together — one step at a time — into a life that is stronger, freer, and truly limitless.

Declaration

Today I choose faith over fear, purpose over passivity, and obedience over opinion.
I am not defined by limits or labels—I am defined by the God who called me.
His strength flows through my weakness; His grace crowns my effort with impact.
My words build, my hands serve, my heart stays soft and my spine stays strong.
I plant what I want multiplied: courage, kindness, truth, and holy joy.
I move at heaven's pace and still arrive on time.
Doors meant for me open; what is not for me fades without regret.
I carry light into every room and leave it brighter than I found it.
I forgive quickly, love loudly, and lead with integrity—seen or unseen.
My life is a living letter and my legacy is love in action.
By God's power, I will finish faithfully and begin boldly—again and again.
So help me God—let my yes echo for generations.

CHAPTER 1

The Power of Faith In The Face of Limitation

What Are Limitations, and How Do They Show Up in Our Lives?

Life is beautiful, but it is also filled with battles — and often those battles show up in the form of limitations. Some are visible: a health crisis, financial strain, broken relationships, or dreams that always seem out of reach. Others are invisible: self-doubt, fear, insecurity, and the quiet inner whisper that tells us we are not enough.

Limitations wear many disguises. They can be physical — an illness that weakens the body, an injury that slows us down, or simply the effects of time. They can be financial — the weight of debt, the struggle of lack, or the frustration of not having enough resources. And they can be emotional or mental — fears that paralyze us, insecurities that silence us, or mental blocks that keep us trapped in cycles of "I can't."

But here's the truth: limitations do not define us — unless we allow them to.

I know this firsthand. One day, my voice — the very thing I had relied on my whole life — vanished. No warning. No explanation. Doctors couldn't find a reason, and I was left staring into silence. My identity felt stripped away. Who was I without my voice? How could I share my heart? How could I be heard?

The weight of that loss felt unbearable. But slowly, I discovered something life-changing: I am not my limitation. And neither are you. What holds us back is not the obstacle itself, but the belief that the obstacle has the final word.

Building Faith: The Tool That Breaks Through Barriers

Faith is not passive. It's not just nodding to the unseen. Faith is active. Faith is alive. Faith is the force that allows us to push through walls that should have crushed us.

When I stood in silence, stripped of my voice, faith became my anchor. It steadied me when fear and despair tried to pull me under. Faith wasn't just believing God existed; it was trusting that He had the power to turn my brokenness into beauty.

Faith is the lens that allows us to see beyond the fog of our limitations. It whispers, *"This is not the end. This is a stepping stone."* Faith bridges the gap between where we are and where we are meant to be.

Faith in Scripture: Timeless Lessons

The Bible is filled with reminders of what happens when ordinary people put extraordinary faith in God.

- **David and Goliath (1 Samuel 17):** A shepherd boy faced a warrior giant with nothing but a sling and a stone. But it wasn't his weapon that secured the victory — it was his unshakable faith that the God of Israel was bigger than the giant in front of him.

- **The Woman with the Issue of Blood (Mark 5:25-34):** For twelve long years, she suffered. Weak, isolated, and without answers, she still believed that one touch of Jesus' garment would heal her. And it did. Jesus told her, *"Daughter, your faith has healed you."*

Both stories remind us that faith does not ignore reality — it simply declares that God's power is greater than the reality we face.

Faith in Real Life: My Testimony

My journey of losing my voice taught me that faith doesn't remove the struggle — it empowers us to endure, to rise, and to be transformed in the middle of it. I stopped asking, *"Why me?"* and started asking, *"God, what do You want to teach me here?"*

And little by little, I saw His hand at work. The silence that once felt like a prison became a classroom for resilience, trust, and purpose. My limitation didn't end my story; it rewrote it.

Your Turn: Reflecting on Your Own Limitations

What limitation are you facing right now? Is it financial? Emotional? Relational? Physical? Maybe it's not visible to the world, but it's weighing heavily on you.

Don't ignore it. Acknowledge it — but don't stop there. Lay it before God. Pray. Fill your mind with His promises:

- *"For nothing will be impossible with God."* (Luke 1:37)
- *"I can do all things through Christ who strengthens me."* (Philippians 4:13)
- *"With man this is impossible, but with God all things are possible."* (Matthew 19:26)

Let these truths reshape your perspective. Take small steps of faith. Reach out. Pursue the dream again. Believe again.

Faith Beyond Limits

Faith doesn't deny the struggle. Faith declares that the struggle cannot stop us. With faith, we can look at our giants and declare, *"You will fall."* We can reach for Jesus and believe, *"I will be healed."*

Your limitations do not define you. **The limitless God who walks with you defines you.** And with Him, there is no ceiling, no barrier, no chain that cannot be broken.

This is the power of faith in the face of limitations: it transforms barriers into bridges, setbacks into setups, and endings into beginnings.

Now it's your turn to rise with faith beyond limits — because your story is still being written, and God has greater chapters ahead.

Affirmation for Faith Beyond Limits

"I am not defined by my limitations. My faith in God gives me strength, courage, and clarity. With every step I take in trust, I rise above obstacles, walk in freedom, and move closer to the life God has destined for me."

Reflection: The Power of Faith In The Face of Limitations

Naming Your Giants
- What limitations are you currently facing (physical, emotional, financial, relational, or spiritual)?
- How have these challenges shaped the way you see yourself?

Faith vs. Fear
- When you think about your current struggle, what does fear say to you?
- Now, what does faith in God say in response? Write both down and compare them.

God's Track Record
- Recall a time when God helped you overcome something you thought was impossible.

- How does remembering His faithfulness give you confidence to face today's challenges?

Reframing Your Limitation
- How can you view your current limitation not as a barrier, but as an opportunity for God to reveal His power?

Action in Faith
- What one small step of faith can you take this week to move beyond your limitation? (Prayer, conversation, new opportunity, act of courage?)

CHAPTER 2

Embracing Your Struggles as Catalysts for Growth

Struggles Are Not Roadblocks, They're Stepping Stones

Life often feels like a relentless storm — one challenge after another, leaving us weary, uncertain, and questioning what's ahead. But what if the very struggles that feel like chains are actually the chisels shaping you? What if your pain is not punishment, but preparation?

Struggles are uncomfortable, inconvenient, and often heartbreaking. They force us to face parts of ourselves we would rather avoid — fear, vulnerability, insecurity, weakness. Yet, every challenge carries within it the seed of transformation. Struggles are not the end of your story; they are the beginning of a greater chapter God is writing.

The key is perspective. Instead of viewing struggles as immovable roadblocks, we must begin to see them as invitations — invitations to grow stronger, to deepen our faith, to discover who we really are, and to embrace the life God is calling us toward.

My Journey: Finding God in the Struggle

A few years ago, I was stopped in my tracks by a health battle I could neither predict nor prevent. My body betrayed me. Suddenly, I couldn't do the things I loved, I couldn't keep up the pace I was used to, and I couldn't even leave home without help. I felt trapped in my own skin.

At first, I was angry. I fought hard against the reality of my condition, determined to push through by sheer willpower. But the more I resisted, the worse it became. Finally, I reached a breaking point — flat on my back, exhausted, and in tears.

That's when I cried out to God: *"Why me? What good could possibly come from this?"* And in that still moment of surrender, I felt a quiet whisper in my spirit: *"I have something for you in this. Trust Me."*

It wasn't the instant healing I wanted, but it was the beginning of something greater. My struggle became my teacher. In the silence, I learned to listen. In the pain, I discovered patience. In the helplessness, I found new strength. My illness didn't just weaken me — it revealed the places where God's power could shine the brightest.

Turning Pain into Purpose

There's a truth I've come to hold onto with all my heart: no pain is wasted when God is in control.

The Apostle Paul knew this well. In 2 Corinthians 12:9, God told him, **"My grace is sufficient for you, for my power is made perfect in weakness."** Paul responded not with despair, but with confidence, saying that he would "boast all the more gladly" in his weaknesses so that Christ's power could rest upon him.

Your struggle is not the end — it's the setup for transformation. God doesn't waste your tears, your setbacks, or your silent nights of wrestling. He turns them into tools, shaping you into the person He designed you to be.

Struggles strip away illusions of control and force us to anchor ourselves in what truly matters. They deepen our faith, sharpen our vision, and strengthen our character. They remind us that our strength was never enough — but God's strength has no limit.

Finding Growth in Your Own Struggles

Take a moment to reflect on the battles you're facing right now:

- What struggle feels like it's weighing you down the most?
- What emotions has it stirred in you — fear, anger, hopelessness?
- Can you see any areas of growth that have already come from this hardship?
- How might this very challenge be shaping you into the person God has called you to be?

Write your answers. Be honest. And then ask God to reveal how He might be using your pain to prepare you for purpose.

Faith That Redefines Struggles

The truth is, growth rarely comes in seasons of comfort. It comes through fire, through pressure, through struggles that test us to our core. But when we look through the lens of faith, we see struggles differently.

Romans 5:3-4 reminds us: **"We also glory in our sufferings, because we know that suffering produces perseverance; perseverance, character; and character, hope."**

Your struggles are not wasted. They are producing strength, character, and hope in you. They are refining you, not destroying you.

The Invitation of Struggle

Every struggle whispers a question: *Will this break you, or will this build you?*

The answer lies in your response. You can allow struggles to trap you in bitterness and defeat, or you can choose to see them as the very ground where God grows your purpose.

My struggles didn't end my story. They refined it. And the same is true for you. Your challenges are not signs of failure; they are proof that you are being prepared for something greater.

So, embrace the struggle. Lean into it. Trust God in it. Because every tear, every setback, and every hard season is shaping you for your calling.

Remember: **Your struggles don't define you. God does. And in His hands, your pain becomes the soil where your purpose takes root.**

Affirmation for Faith Beyond Limits

"My struggles are not breaking me, they are building me. Every challenge is shaping my character, strengthening my faith, and preparing me for the greater purpose God has designed for me. No pain is wasted — it all works together for my growth and transformation."

Reflection: Turning Struggles Into Growth

Facing the Struggle Honestly

- What struggle am I currently facing that feels like a roadblock?
- How have I been viewing this struggle — as punishment, inconvenience, or as an opportunity for growth?

Shifting Perspective

- In what ways could this challenge be refining me — building resilience, teaching patience, or deepening my faith?
- What lessons has this struggle already revealed about who I am and who God is in my life?

Purpose in the Pain

- How might God be using this struggle to prepare me for a greater calling or purpose?
- Can I identify moments where past struggles ended up opening unexpected doors or revealing hidden strengths?

Faith in Action

- What small step of faith can I take today to embrace this struggle as a catalyst instead of resisting it?
- How can I turn my personal pain into encouragement for someone else who may be walking a similar path?

Living Victoriously

- When I think about Romans 5:3-4 ("*suffering produces perseverance; perseverance, character; and character, hope*"), what character traits might God be building in me through this season?
- How can I remind myself daily that my struggles are temporary, but the growth they produce is eternal?

CHAPTER 3

Trusting In God's Timing

Learning to Trust Beyond the Clock

We live in a world that thrives on speed. Instant messages, fast food, next-day delivery — everything around us teaches us that waiting is wasted time. So, when life asks us to wait, especially when it comes to prayers we've poured our heart into, it can feel unbearable.

Whether it's waiting for healing, a financial breakthrough, the right relationship, or the fulfillment of a dream, the pause between *what we prayed for* and *what God promised* can test the strongest faith. Our human nature craves control. We want it now, and when it doesn't happen, frustration rises. But here's the truth: our timeline is not God's timeline. And His timing is always perfect.

Human time is measured in minutes, days, and years. But God is not bound by the ticking of a clock. He sees the bigger picture — the beginning, the end, and everything in between. What feels delayed to us is often preparation in disguise.

When Waiting Becomes a Teacher

Waiting is not passive; it's an active surrender. It's the space where God refines us, stretches us, and prepares us for what's ahead. Yet, we often resist the very process designed to strengthen us.

When I lost my ability to speak, I begged for instant healing. I wanted a miracle on demand — a quick restoration so I could go back to "normal." Each silent day felt like rejection. But God wasn't ignoring me. He was teaching me. In the silence, I learned to listen. In the waiting, I discovered patience. My voice returned — but by then, I was not the same. I had been reshaped by the delay. My healing was deeper than my throat; it was in my spirit.

Sometimes God's greatest answers are not about fixing the situation immediately, but about forming something eternal in us during the wait.

The Anchor of Scripture

God's Word is filled with reminders that His timing is not ours, but it is always right:

- *"To everything there is a season, a time for every purpose under heaven."* (Ecclesiastes 3:1)
- *"And we know that in all things God works for the good of those who love Him."* (Romans 8:28)
- *"As the heavens are higher than the earth, so are my ways higher than your ways and my thoughts than your thoughts."* (Isaiah 55:8-9)

These verses remind us: nothing is wasted. No delay is meaningless. Every season — even the long ones — serves a greater purpose in God's plan.

From Impatience to Surrender

The truth is, delays test us. They expose where we've been relying on ourselves instead of God. But they also invite us into freedom. Because when we let go of control, we make space for peace.

Ask yourself:

- Where am I growing impatient?
- What have I been trying to force in my own strength?
- How can I shift from frustration to trust?

Impatience says, *"It's taking too long."* Faith says, *"God is still working, even in the silence."*

The Gift of God's Timing

God's timing is never about convenience; it's about purpose. Consider Abraham and Sarah, who waited decades for the promised child. When Isaac finally arrived, it wasn't too early, it wasn't too late — it was right on time. Their waiting became the testimony that God's promises never fail.

The same is true for us. God's timing is not random; it's deliberate. It protects us, prepares us, and positions us for blessings we couldn't handle any earlier. The delay is not denial. It's development.

Living with Peace in the Waiting

Here's how you can begin to walk in trust when your patience runs thin:

1. **Be Honest About Impatience** – Admit to God when you're frustrated. He can handle it.
2. **Pray with Surrender** – Shift from "God, do this now" to "God, have Your way in me."
3. **Remember His Faithfulness** – Reflect on past seasons when His timing turned out to be perfect.

4. **Stay Faithful Where You Are** – Use the waiting season to serve, grow, and prepare.
5. **Anchor in His Promises** – Remind yourself daily: *God has not forgotten me. He is at work.*

Why His Timing Is Always Worth It

Trusting God's timing is not easy, but it is always worth it. What feels like a painful pause today will one day become the story you share of His faithfulness. You'll look back and see how the waiting built your character, deepened your faith, and prepared you for blessings beyond what you imagined.

God is never late. He is always on time. Always.

So, take a deep breath. Release your timeline. And trust that the Author of time itself knows exactly what He's doing.

Affirmation for Faith Beyond Limits

"I release my need to control the timeline of my life. I trust that God's timing is always perfect, even when I cannot see the full picture. I choose peace over impatience, surrender over striving, and faith over fear. What God has planned for me will come to pass — not a moment too soon or too late, but right on time."

Reflection: Living in Alignment with God's Timing

Recognizing My Waiting Season

- What am I currently waiting for that feels delayed or out of reach?
- How has my impatience been shaping my perspective in this season?

Learning in the Delay

- What lessons could God be teaching me while I wait?
- How has this season already refined my patience, trust, or faith?

Surrendering Control

- What areas of my life am I still trying to control instead of entrusting to God?
- How can I practice releasing those areas into His hands today?

Looking Back, Building Faith

- When has God's timing in the past proven better than my own?
- How can I use that memory to strengthen my trust in Him now?

Shifting My Response

- Instead of asking *"Why is this taking so long?"* what new question of faith can I ask God in this season?
- What daily practice (prayer, journaling, scripture, gratitude) can I lean into while I wait?

CHAPTER 4

Overcoming Self-Doubt and Embracing Your True Identity

The Lie of Self-Doubt: Breaking Free to Walk in God's Fullness

There's a voice that creeps in, soft but sharp—the voice of doubt. It whispers, *"You're not enough. You're too weak. You're unworthy of the vision burning inside you."* That voice is a liar. It is the lie of self-doubt, and if you let it, it will chain your feet, dim your fire, and keep you from stepping into the breathtaking fullness of what God has designed for your life.

Self-doubt is a thief dressed in disguise. It robs you quietly—first your confidence, then your courage, and then your calling. It tricks you into trading boldness for timidity, purpose for passivity, and destiny for defeat. Before you know it, you've shrunk into a smaller version of yourself, settling for crumbs when God already set a banquet before you.

But hear this truth: self-doubt is not from God. It is the enemy's favorite weapon—a counterfeit narrative meant to paralyze you. He wants you tangled in fear, convinced you're too flawed, too broken, too unworthy. But the Word of God declares something radically different. It declares that you are fearfully and wonderfully made. You are chosen. Appointed. Equipped. Loved beyond measure. God has already signed His "yes" over your life, and no lie of doubt can erase His truth.

When you bow to self-doubt, you build walls where God meant to open doors. You miss opportunities He hand-carved for your breakthrough. You silence your own voice when heaven is waiting for your roar. But when you call self-doubt by its name—a bold-faced lie—you break its power. You rise. You reclaim your identity as a daughter of the King, clothed in strength, armed with purpose, and unstoppable in faith.

Beloved, your life is not meant to be lived in the shadows of doubt. You are meant to blaze trails, carry light, and walk boldly in the inheritance of God's promises. Shake off the lie. Stand tall in your true identity. The fullness of God's plan is waiting, and the only thing you'll regret is the time you wasted believing the lie instead of walking in the truth.

God's Truth About You: Loved, Chosen, and Empowered

If self-doubt is the enemy's lie, then God's truth is the weapon that shatters it. The surest way to silence the voice of fear is to embrace the voice of God—the voice that declares who you really are. When you anchor your identity in His love, His choice, and His empowerment, you step into a confidence that hell itself cannot shake.

You Are Loved Beyond Measure

First and foremost, hear this: you are loved by God. Not because you've performed well. Not because you've earned it. Simply because He has chosen to set His love on you. His love is unconditional, unshakable, and unstoppable. Paul wrote in Romans 8:38-39 that nothing—not death, not demons, not your past, not your failures, not your future mistakes—*nothing* can separate you from the love of God in Christ Jesus. That means you don't have to hustle for worth. You don't have to perform for acceptance. You are already valued, already treasured, already embraced. His love is the foundation that gives your life weight, beauty, and purpose.

You Are Chosen on Purpose, With Purpose

You are not an accident. You are not an afterthought. Before the first sunrise lit the earth,

God already had you in mind. Ephesians 1:4-5 tells us He chose you before the creation of the world. He called you holy, blameless, adopted into His family, and destined for greatness in His Kingdom. That means your life is intentional. Your gifts are intentional. Your struggles, even, are woven into a greater story. When you doubt yourself, remember: God didn't. He saw you before you were formed and said, *"That one—I've got a mission for her."*

You Are Empowered to Do the Impossible

God never calls you without equipping you. The same Spirit that raised Jesus from the dead is alive in you right now. That's why Paul boldly declared in 2 Timothy 1:7: ***"For the Spirit God gave us does not make us timid, but gives us power, love and self-discipline."*** You have power. You have divine love. You have discipline rooted in His Spirit. Fear doesn't define you. Insecurity doesn't own you. You carry within you the resources of heaven to fulfill every assignment on your life.

Breaking Limiting Beliefs

Self-doubt breeds limiting beliefs—those inner narratives that whisper, *"I'm not good enough… I'm too broken… I'll never succeed."* But those are lies. Here's how to dismantle them:

1. **Recognize the Belief** → Name the lies you've been carrying.

2. **Challenge It** → Ask: Does this align with God's Word or the enemy's deception? Replace lies with truth (Psalm 139:14, Philippians 4:13).
3. **Affirm the Truth** → Declare: *"I am loved. I am chosen. I am empowered."* Say it until your spirit rises in agreement.
4. **Seek Support** → Walk with people who speak life and truth, not doubt and fear. Iron sharpens iron.

Real Stories, Real Breakthroughs

I remember the days when doubt nearly drowned me. Every time I dreamed of writing, speaking, or launching a business, a chorus of lies rose up: *"Who do you think you are? You'll fail. You're not enough."* But then I started speaking God's truth out loud. I surrounded myself with encouragers who reminded me of the call of God on my life. Step by trembling step, I moved forward. And every act of obedience silenced another lie. Today, I walk in the calling I once feared, and I know this: God's truth always outshines self-doubt. And I've watched it happen for others too—friends who stepped into businesses, ministries, and creative callings after years of fear. Once they realized failure doesn't define them—faith does—they began to soar.

Moving Beyond Doubt

You may hear voices whisper: *"You're unqualified... You've failed too much... You're unworthy... You don't know where to start."* But these are not truths—they are chains. And chains were made to be broken.

The Word of God says:

- You are **qualified** because God equips the called (Exodus 3:11).
- You are **redeemed**, not disqualified by your past (1 Samuel 16:7).
- You are **worthy**, because Christ made you worthy (Romans 5:8).
- You are **guided**, even when you don't see the whole path (Psalm 119:105).

Stepping Into Freedom

To embrace your true identity:

1. Identify the lies.
2. Replace them with Scripture.
3. Speak God's truth daily.
4. Take action even while afraid—faith grows in motion.
5. Surround yourself with truth-tellers who remind you of who you are.

Angela Gadiare

Beloved, you are not defined by self-doubt. You are defined by God's unshakable truth: you are loved, chosen, and empowered. When you walk in this reality, nothing can stop you from fulfilling the divine destiny written over your life.

Affirmation for Faith Beyond Limits

"I am loved without condition, chosen with intention, and empowered by God's Spirit. I reject the lies of self-doubt and walk boldly in my true identity—worthy, equipped, and unstoppable in Christ."

Reflection: Overcoming Self-Doubt and Embracing Your True Identity

- **Loved by God** – His love is steady, unshakable, and not based on performance. Rest in the truth that nothing can separate you from His embrace.

- **Chosen for Purpose** – You are not an accident; your life carries divine assignment. Every step you take is evidence that God planned you for impact.

- **Empowered by the Spirit** – God's Spirit within you is greater than fear, stronger than doubt, and powerful enough to carry you into victory.

- **Replacing Limiting Beliefs** – Lies lose their grip when God's Word takes center stage. Trade every "I can't" for His eternal "You can."

- **Daily Practice** – Speak life into your atmosphere. With each declaration, you are rewriting your story and aligning with heaven's blueprint for you.

CHAPTER 5

The Importance of Serving Beyond Yourself

The Power of Service: Shifting Focus from Self to God's Work

The world teaches us to chase *me, mine, and more*. But heaven teaches a different rhythm: the secret to fulfillment is found not in climbing ladders, but in lifting others. Service is the great refocus—it pulls our eyes off our limits and places them on the limitless work of God.

When we serve, we stop magnifying obstacles and start magnifying the One who works through us. The miracle? As we bless others, God transforms us. Our weakness becomes strength, our emptiness becomes overflow, and our life aligns with eternal purpose.

Jesus said in Matthew 10:39: **"Whoever finds their life will lose it, and whoever loses their life for my sake will find it."** True life is discovered when we stop living only for ourselves and begin living as vessels for God's Kingdom.

The Example of Jesus: The Servant King

Jesus—the Son of God—came not to be served, but to serve. He healed the sick, fed the hungry, comforted the broken, and even washed the dusty feet of His disciples. Foot washing was the lowest servant's job, yet the King of Kings knelt and did it. In John 13:12-15 He declared: ***"I have set you an example that you should do as I have done for you."*** His service wasn't about recognition. It was about love, humility, and obedience. His cross was the ultimate act of service—a reminder that greatness isn't about titles but about sacrifice.

Serving in Your Limitations

You may feel too tired, too overwhelmed, or too broken to serve. But here's the truth: God doesn't need your perfection—He desires your willingness. Service is most powerful when it flows from vulnerability.

Serving doesn't always mean grand gestures. Sometimes it's:

- Sending a text to encourage a weary soul.
- Sharing a meal with someone who feels forgotten.

- Offering your talents—writing, cooking, organizing—to bless others.
- Listening with compassion when someone just needs to be heard.

No act of service is too small when offered with a grateful heart.

Practical Ways to Serve

1. **Start Small** – Let your service be simple but sincere.
2. **Volunteer Time** – At church, in your community, or wherever God opens a door.
3. **Serve by Listening** – Presence often matters more than solutions.
4. **Use Your Gifts** – Your skills are divine tools for Kingdom impact.
5. **Serve with Gratitude** – Joyful service reflects the heart of God.

Self-Reflection: Where Am I Serving?

- Where am I already serving others?
- Where can I serve more deeply or consistently?
- How can I stretch beyond my comfort zone?

Action Step: Choose one new area to serve this week—whether small or bold—and commit to it.

Breaking Barriers to Service

Sometimes fear, pride, or feelings of inadequacy hold us back. Ask yourself:

- Do I believe my service won't matter?
- Am I afraid of failing or being unseen?
- Do I feel I lack time or resources?

Action Step: Identify one barrier and challenge it. Take one small act of service in faith.

Serving as Worship

Colossians 3:23 reminds us: ***"Whatever you do, work at it with all your heart, as working for the Lord..."***

When we serve, we aren't just meeting needs—we're worshiping. Every meal given, every prayer whispered, every hand extended is a song of love to the Lord.

The Call to Serve

Serving isn't about what we gain—it's about what we give. It's not about being flawless—it's about being faithful. When you serve others, you're not just changing their lives—you're changing yours. Even in your limitations, you have something to offer. And when you offer it, God multiplies it.

Remember this: Service shifts the story. It transforms self-doubt into purpose, scarcity into abundance, and ordinary acts into eternal impact.

Affirmation for Faith Beyond Limits

"I am called, equipped, and empowered to serve. My life is not limited by my weaknesses but expanded by God's strength working through me. Every act of service I give reflects His love, multiplies His grace, and fulfills His purpose in my life."

Reflection: The Importance of Serving Beyond Yourself

- **Shift Your Focus** – Where am I looking inward too much, and how can serving others help me lift my eyes to God's bigger picture?

- **Jesus as My Model** – How does Christ's example of washing feet challenge me to embrace humility in my own service?

- **Small Acts, Big Impact** – What simple act of kindness can I do this week that might ripple farther than I realize?

- **Breaking Barriers** – What fear, doubt, or excuse has been holding me back from serving more boldly, and how will I overcome it?

- **Serving as Worship** – How can I reframe my daily tasks, even the ordinary ones, as acts of worship to God?

CHAPTER 6

Navigating the Valley of the Shadow of Death

When the Valley Finds You

Hard seasons don't RSVP. They don't knock politely or wait for a convenient moment. They barge in uninvited—illness, loss, financial strain, the ache of anxiety—and suddenly the air feels thin, heavy, almost unbreathable. You don't choose the valley; the valley chooses you. And when it does, every step feels like it takes all the strength you've got left.

In those moments, your heart whispers the questions no one likes to admit: *Will I make it to morning? Will I ever see joy again? Is there really a way out?* Yes. You will. Not because the valley is small, but because God is greater than the valley. Not because you are strong enough, but because His strength will not fail you.

"Even though I walk through the darkest valley, I will fear no evil, for You are with me; Your rod and Your staff, they comfort me." — Psalm 23:4

Notice that David doesn't say *if* I walk through the valley; he says *when*. Valleys are inevitable. But valleys are not final. They are not your grave—they are your passage. And here's the truth: valleys have shadows only because there is light nearby. A shadow means the sun still shines, even if you can't see it directly. God's presence is the light that casts out fear.

You may feel weak, but God is not. You may feel abandoned, but God draws near. In the hours when answers hide, His nearness becomes the answer. He does not promise you'll never face valleys, but He does promise this: you will not walk them alone. When the valley finds you, don't forget—God's rod guides, His staff protects, and His presence comforts. What feels like the end is often the very place where God begins to write a new chapter of your story.

Presence in the Dark

Darkness has a way of convincing us that we've been abandoned, that our cries have gone unheard. Yet Scripture shouts the opposite: God is closest in the silence, most present in the shadows.

"The Lord is close to the brokenhearted and saves those who are crushed in spirit." — Psalm 34:18

His presence is not always dramatic—it may be a peace you can't explain, a friend's timely encouragement, a Scripture that leaps off the page when you needed it most. The enemy wants you to believe that if you don't feel God, He must not be there. But feelings are not the evidence—faith is.

God's presence in the dark is like a lantern: it doesn't always light the whole path, but it gives enough glow for the next step. And that's all you need to keep walking. He does not vanish when circumstances grow grim—He draws nearer.

Fire That Refines

Nobody volunteers for the fire. But the fire is where faith matures. Trials don't arrive to annihilate you; they arrive to purify you.

"Consider it pure joy, my brothers and sisters, whenever you face trials of many kinds, because you know that the testing of your faith produces perseverance." — James 1:2–3

Like gold in the furnace, impurities rise in the heat: impatience, pride, control, fear. And slowly, what emerges is purer faith—faith that doesn't break when the ground shakes, faith that has roots deep enough to weather storms. This refining isn't punishment; it's preparation. God doesn't allow the fire to destroy you, but to strip away what was never meant to define you. You come out not weaker, but stronger, more resilient, and more anchored in Him.

When you're in the fire, it feels endless. But when you emerge, you'll discover what Shadrach, Meshach, and Abednego did in Daniel 3: **the flames may touch you, but they cannot consume you when God is in the fire with you.**

Promises That Hold

Fear is loud. Promises are louder—if you'll let them be. Scripture is not poetic filler; it is oxygen for suffocating souls.

"So do not fear, for I am with you; do not be dismayed, for I am your God. I will strengthen you and help you." — Isaiah 41:10

When the valley whispers, "You're alone," promises shout, "I will never leave you nor forsake you."

When the valley sneers, "You won't make it," promises declare, "You are more than a conqueror through Christ."

When the valley hisses, "You're not strong enough," promises roar, "My strength is made perfect in weakness."

God's promises are not fragile—they are iron-clad covenants. Write them. Speak them. Pray them. Hold them like a lifeline. Because that's exactly what they are.

Hope Has A Future

Hope is oxygen in the valley. Without it, despair chokes out the will to keep moving. But biblical hope is not wishful thinking—it's confident expectation rooted in God's faithfulness. Job lost everything, yet declared, "I know that my Redeemer lives." Joseph endured betrayal and prison, only to discover his pain positioned him for purpose. Jesus endured the cross, trusting the resurrection waiting on the other side.

"Suffering produces perseverance; perseverance, character; and character, hope. And hope does not put us to shame." — Romans 5:3–5

Hope anchors you when the storm rages. Hope reminds you that valleys are passages, not prisons. Hope points you to the God who turns graves into gardens, mourning into dancing, ashes into beauty. Cling to hope, even if it feels like a whisper. Sometimes hope is not a roar but a seed—and seeds, when planted in faith, grow into forests.

How to Walk Through (Not Camp In) the Valley

The valley is meant to be walked through, not settled in. Here's how to keep moving when you'd rather curl up and quit:

- **Name the pain.**

    Denial doesn't heal. Honesty invites God's comfort. Lament like David—pour it out raw. Healing begins with truth.

- **Choose trust over clarity.**

    You may never understand every why, but you can trust the Who. Trust is not passive; it's active surrender—saying, "God, I don't get it, but I give it to You."

- **Feed on promises daily.**

    Your faith diet matters. Replace constant replay of your fears with constant replay of God's Word. His promises are fuel; without them, you'll run on empty.

- **Borrow strength from community.**

    Even Jesus didn't carry His cross alone— Simon of Cyrene helped. Don't try to carry yours in isolation. Invite people to pray, encourage, and walk with you.

- **Move one faithful step at a time.**

    Faith doesn't demand giant leaps; it celebrates small steps. Make the call. Pray the prayer. Open the Bible. Show up. Every small step is proof you're still walking.

- **Worship in the dark.**

    Worship changes the atmosphere. It doesn't deny pain—it declares God's presence above pain. When you sing in the valley, the valley echoes with heaven's voice.

The valley may be long, but it is not endless. You are not abandoned; you are accompanied. You are not undone; you are being refined. God is with you, God is for you, and God is working—even here, even now.

Affirmation for Faith Beyond Limits

"I am called, equipped, and empowered to serve. My life is not limited by my weaknesses but expanded by God's strength working through me. Every act of service I give reflects His love, multiplies His grace, and fulfills His purpose in my life."

Reflection: For The Valley

- The valley is real, but so is God's nearness. In my hardest moments, I can lean into His presence instead of my pain.
- Shadows cannot exist without light—my valley is proof that God's light is still shining.
- The fire of adversity is not here to destroy me; it is here to refine me and reveal the gold of my faith.
- Every promise of God is a thread I can hold onto when the darkness feels overwhelming.
- Hope is not wishful thinking—it is the anchor that tells my soul I will see

resurrection, restoration, and redemption.

- o Valleys are passages, not prisons. With every step, I am walking closer to the mountaintop God has prepared for me.

CHAPTER 7

Walking Boldly In The Call of God

Answering God's Call, Even When You Feel Inadequate

There's nothing casual about the call of God—it interrupts, disrupts, and redirects. It's the moment your "ordinary" collides with His extraordinary. Yet so often, when His whisper comes, our first instinct is resistance. We count our flaws instead of His faithfulness. We replay our past instead of receiving His promise.

Inadequacy will scream louder than destiny if you let it. *"What if I fail? What if I'm not enough? What if someone else could do this better?"* Those questions haunt us. But here's what they forget: it's not your résumé God is scanning—it's your heart. He doesn't call the equipped; He equips the called. His invitation is not about your perfection but about your willingness.

The call is always bigger than you because it's meant to showcase Him. It's designed to stretch your faith, pull you out of comfort, and make you utterly dependent on His Spirit. Obedience doesn't always silence fear, but it does unlock favor. Every time you say yes, you trade self-sufficiency for divine sufficiency.

Presence That Overrides Fear

Fear has a voice, but it doesn't get the final say. God's presence does. When Moses panicked at the burning bush, his inadequacy rose like smoke, but God's reply was steady: *"I will be with you."* (Exodus 3:12). Notice He didn't give Moses a strategy first—He gave him Himself.

That's God's pattern: His presence is the answer to every fear. When Joshua trembled before leading Israel into the Promised Land, God declared, *"Do not be afraid... for the Lord your God will be with you wherever you go."* (Joshua 1:9). When Gideon doubted his ability, God promised, *"I will be with you, and you will strike down the Midianites."* (Judges 6:16).

God doesn't remove fear by inflating our confidence; He removes fear by revealing His presence. Boldness doesn't mean you never feel afraid—it means you don't let fear set the terms of your obedience. The presence of God turns *"What if I can't?"* into *"Watch what He can."*

Power In Weakness

The Kingdom flips human logic upside down. We celebrate strength, but God celebrates surrender. Paul captured this paradox when he wrote, ***"For when I am weak, then I am strong."*** (2 Corinthians 12:10). Weakness isn't your disqualification; it's your qualification for grace.

Think of David—too young, overlooked, underestimated. Yet it was David's sling, not Saul's sword, that toppled Goliath. Think of Peter—impulsive, unstable, quick to deny. Yet it was Peter who preached with fire at Pentecost, leading thousands to Christ. Their weakness didn't diminish God's call—it magnified His glory.

When you embrace weakness, you allow God to display His strength in a way that no human effort could imitate. Your scars, insecurities, and failures become altars where His power rests. That's why you can walk boldly—not because you have it all together, but because He holds it all together.

From Hesitation To Boldness: Lessons from the Called

- **Moses** shows us that self-doubt cannot cancel destiny. He felt tongue-tied, yet God's words shook empires. His story proves that availability outweighs ability.

- **Esther** shows us that courage often feels like trembling. She risked her life before a king, but Heaven's King backed her obedience. She teaches us that your position is not random; it's providence.
- **Paul** shows us that your past does not disqualify you from God's future. From persecutor to preacher, his life screams grace. He teaches us that God doesn't waste a single detail of our story—not even the ugly parts.

Each of these lives declares a timeless truth: God doesn't need flawless vessels; He uses willing ones. Boldness isn't born from self-confidence—it's born from God-confidence.

Practical Steps for Walking Boldly

- **Trust God, Not Yourself**

  Stop magnifying your limitations. God doesn't need your strength; He needs your surrender. When He called Jeremiah, the prophet cried out, *"I am too young!"* God answered, *"Do not say, 'I am too young'... I have put My words in your mouth."* (Jeremiah 1:7,9). Trust His sufficiency, not your scarcity.

- **Start Small, Step Now**

  Don't wait for the giant stage—faith grows in small yeses. Teach the one, serve the few, write the first page, say the first prayer. Bold obedience begins in hidden places, and God multiplies it in time.

- **Surround Yourself with Support**

    Every bold calling needs a circle of encouragement. Moses had Aaron. Esther had Mordecai. Paul had Barnabas. Find those who fuel your faith, not feed your fear.

- **Hold Tight to God's Promises**

    Your call will face storms. Anchor yourself in Scripture. Write His promises on sticky notes, walls, journals—wherever fear tries to rise. His Word isn't just encouragement; it's equipment.

- **Don't Wait for Perfection**

    Perfectionism is procrastination in disguise. If you wait to feel "ready," you'll never move. God blesses motion, not hesitation. Step trembling if you must—just step.

A Personal Note

I once stood in front of an assignment that felt too heavy for my flawed hands. I wanted to retreat. Yet as I stepped out trembling, I discovered that God doesn't anoint our comfort zones—He anoints our obedience. Every time I said yes, my confidence didn't grow in me—it grew in Him. And here's the miracle: He didn't just use my yes to bless others; He used it to transform me.

Walking Boldly Today

This isn't just about ministry. It's about family, motherhood, leadership, community, business, relationships—wherever God's voice intersects your life. His call is woven into your daily rhythm and into your biggest dreams. Saying yes today opens doors you can't see yet.

The call of God isn't optional; it's destiny. When you rise to it, Heaven backs you. When you walk in it, generations are changed. The world doesn't need a perfect you—it needs a willing you. And when you walk boldly in His call, you carry Kingdom impact with every step.

Affirmation for Faith Beyond Limits

I am chosen, equipped, and empowered for such a time as this. My weakness is the platform for God's strength. Fear cannot silence me. Doubt cannot stop me. My yes unlocks destiny, and my obedience shifts eternity.

Reflection: Walking Boldly In The Call

- **Presence Over Panic** – God's presence is the guarantee I need. I don't walk alone.

- **Weakness as a Weapon** – My scars tell a story of His strength.

- **Call Over Comfort** – Obedience will always require courage, but courage carries breakthrough.

- **Faith in Action** – Every small yes today paves the way for bigger assignments tomorrow.

- **Impact Beyond Me** – My obedience doesn't stop with me; it impacts generations.

CHAPTER 8

Living A Life Beyond Limitations

Living Fully in Christ: The Abundant Life God Promises

In Christ, abundance isn't a mood—it's your new normal. Jesus didn't save you to squeeze you into a smaller life. He came to unlock a fuller one. **"The thief comes only to steal and kill and destroy; I have come that they may have life, and have it to the full."** (John 10:10, NIV)

Abundant life isn't about trophies, titles, or trouble-free days. It's the deep current of God's power, peace, and purpose running through ordinary moments. It's His strength where you feel weak, His glory shining through your everyday yes.

To live fully in Christ is to let God's promises define you, not your past, your present pressure, or your self-doubt. It's not perfection—it's obedience. Not self-reliance—it's trust.

"**My grace is sufficient for you, for My power is made perfect in weakness.**" (2 Corinthians 12:9) "**Exceedingly, abundantly above all we ask or imagine.**" (Ephesians 3:20)

Breaking Free from Fear: Failure, Rejection, Inadequacy

Fear is the enemy's favorite leash. God cut it. **"For the Spirit God gave us does not make us timid, but gives us** power, love and self-discipline." (2 Timothy 1:7, NIV)

Your worth isn't up for public vote. It's anchored in Christ—chosen, loved, redeemed. Failures aren't tombstones; they're training grounds. **"For though the righteous fall seven times,** they rise again." (Proverbs 24:16, NIV) Let God turn setbacks into comebacks while you keep moving.

Living Boldly: Step Into Your Purpose

Bold doesn't mean "never scared." Bold means "moved by faith more than fear." Use what God gave you—gifts, gaps, scars, and stories—to serve people and glorify Him.

"What, then, shall we say…? If God is for us, who can be against us?" (Romans 8:31–32, NIV) If He didn't spare His Son, He's not about to starve your purpose. Walk forward. Heaven funds what Heaven authors.

Testimony: Beyond My Limits

I once believed my struggles disqualified me. Health battles, heavy fears—I felt "too broken" for big assignments. But when I stepped anyway, God met me in the "not enough" and turned it into more than enough. My weakness became a window for His power. Obedience—one small step at a time—led me straight into purpose and into people I could help because of what I'd survived, not in spite of it.

Practical Ways to Live Beyond Limitations

- **Pray Boldly**
  Ask specifically. Align with His will. Request courage and clarity. Pray like you expect movement.

- **Speak Truth, Not Limitation**
  Replace mental static with Scripture: "I can do all things through Christ who strengthens me" (Philippians 4:13). Say it daily.

- **Choose Your Circle Wisely**
  Stay close to lifters—people who pray with you, challenge you, and call out the gold in you.

- **Act While Afraid**
  Perfection is a stalling tactic. Start small. One faithful step is greater than a thousand perfect plans.

o **Celebrate Small Wins**

  Every obedient step counts. Mark it. Gratitude builds momentum.

Reflection Exercise: Identify, Confront, Act

- **Name the Limitations**

  Fears, insecurities, old failures—write them down. Be honest.

- **Counter with God's Word**

  Find a verse for each limitation. Let truth talk back to the lie.

- **Take One Bold Step Today**

  Email sent. Call made. Application submitted. Volunteer form filled. Do the next faithful thing

Step-by-Step Guide: Tools for the Journey

Step 1: Identify Your Limitations
Most "walls" are perceived, not permanent.
Action: List them. Then ask, "Is this truly immovable—or movable with God's strength?"

Step 2: Shift Mindset—From Limitation to Possibility
Your thinking steers your life.
Action:
- Write your negative beliefs.
- Reframe with truth (Psalm 139:14, etc.).
- Turn them into daily affirmations you actually say out loud.

Step 3: Break Goals into Micro-Moves
Big visions advance by small hinges.
Action: Deconstruct your biggest goal into next 3 tiny steps. Do step one now.

Step 4: Trust God's Timing
You're not late—you're led.
Action: Pray through your desires. Meditate on Jeremiah 29:11. Journal what obedience looks like this week.

Step 5: Take Brave Action Before You "Feel Ready"
Clarity grows after motion.
Action: Choose one area you've delayed. Commit to a concrete move in the next 24–48 hours.

Deeper Reflections

Limiting Beliefs → Living Truth

- Write the belief.
- Write the Scripture that contradicts it (e.g., Philippians 4:13).
- Note how living that truth would change your next decision.
  Action: Trade one limiting belief for truth each day.

Trusting God's Timing

- Name the anxious areas (career, relationships, growth).
- Sit with Proverbs 3:5–6.
- Identify one act of surrender you'll do today.
  Action: Pray for patience and aligned steps.

Celebrate Small Victories

- Review the past week. List wins, even "tiny."
- Note how God helped.
- Thank Him on purpose.
  Action: Mark one recent win with gratitude (journal, prayer, or a simple treat).

Personal Testimonies

From Fear to Faith

I waited for confidence; God asked for action. One small step flipped the switch—doors opened, resources surfaced, courage followed obedience.

A Journey of Surrender

A career crossroad felt crushing—until I released the outcome. God's timing lined up opportunities I couldn't have engineered if I tried.

Living Beyond Limitations

This doesn't happen overnight. It's a rhythm: trust, act, adjust, repeat. The more you obey, the more you'll see that the "limit" was a launchpad.

God is with you—equipping, guiding, strengthening. Keep moving.

Next Steps (do these now):

- Identify one limitation and take one step past it today.
- Journal your fears and goals; ask God for strength to act in faith.
- Celebrate one win from this week and thank God for it.

You are not defined by fear, failures, or frailty. You are empowered by the Holy Spirit. Walk bold. Walk free. Walk fully—because the One who called you is faithful to equip you for every mile ahead.

Affirmation for Living A Life Beyond Limits

I move by faith, not fear—crowned with courage, carried by God's grace, and unstoppable beyond every limit.

Reflection: Living a Life Beyond Limitations

- **Name the Wall** – What fear, lie, or habit has been limiting me lately? Where do I feel "not enough," and why?

- **Tell the Truth Back** – Which Scripture or promise dismantles that limit? Write it out. How does this truth change the way I approach today?

- **Micro-Move of Faith** – What is one small, concrete action I can take in the next 24–48 hours? What does "obedience, not perfect" look like for me right now?

- **Celebrate the Seed** – List one win from this week—no matter how small. How did God show up in that moment?

- **Vision in Present Tense** – Write 3–4 lines describing yourself living boldly beyond limits—as if it's already true. ("I show up with clarity... I steward my gifts... I serve with joy... I trust God's provision...")

CHAPTER 9

Leaving A Legacy of Faith

Living Beyond Limits, Lighting the Way

Let's tell the truth: trophies tarnish, bank accounts wobble, and even our most dazzling "Ta-da!" moments fade into yesterday's news. But a legacy of faith? That outlives us. That sings after we're gone. That turns our ordinary days into a lighthouse others can steer by.

A legacy of faith isn't about perfection polished to a mirror shine. It's about a life that points past itself—toward the God who does impossible things with very possible people. It's not measured in square footage, followers, or flawless résumés. It's measured in trust, obedience, and love that chooses to show up again and again, especially when the script goes off-book.

What Legacy Really Looks Like

Every choice is a seed. Every act of kindness, every whispered "yes" to God, every courageous step when your knees are knocking—seed. And seeds don't ask permission from the soil; they just grow. The ripples of your faith will lap at shores you'll never see—your children and their children, the neighbor down the hall, the stranger who only watched you from a distance and decided not to give up.

Here's the plot twist: your limitations aren't the disqualifier; they're the stage where God's strength takes the spotlight. He specializes in "I'm not enough" and turns it into "Watch Me work." You don't need to audition for sainthood. God keeps casting ordinary people and stealing the show.

God's Ripple Effect: Small Acts, Wide Waves

Picture a pebble tossed into a calm lake. The circles keep widening long after the splash. That's what obedience does. Abraham didn't see the full sweep of the promise in his lifetime, yet his yes still echoes across the centuries. Faith plants trees we may never sit under. God sees the whole tapestry while we're holding a single thread, wondering if the color fits. Spoiler: it does.

So, take heart—your faithful "today" is already ministering to someone's "tomorrow." When you serve, when you forgive, when you choose hope over hurry and worship over worry, waves form, and God rides them farther than your timeline could imagine.

My Own Ledger of "Yes"

I've known days when illness fogged the road and nights when fear pulled the fire alarm in my chest. I've felt cracked, not collectible; called, yet convinced God might have dialed the wrong number. But grace has a way of slipping through the fractures and making music with the broken bits.

Looking back, what I cherish most isn't the applause or the bullet points on a bio—it's the stubborn trust that wouldn't let me bow out. I want my family, my friends, and even the ones who only know me in passing to say, "God was faithful—and they lived like it." If my imperfect story helps even one weary soul believe that weakness is an entry point, not an exit sign, then that's a legacy worth leaving.

Build as You Go: Legacy in Real Time

Legacy isn't a future monument; it's the footprints you leave between breakfast and bedtime. It's the text you send, the prayer you whisper, the apology you offer, the truth you stand on. It's ordinary obedience with eternal consequences.

So no, you don't need a bigger platform. You need a braver yes. Start where your two feet are standing; God will handle the map.

Legacy Lab: A Guided Reflection

Grab a pen. Breathe. Let's name your impact on purpose.

- **Name the Legacy.**

    What do you want to be remembered for when the noise dims? Write the values that matter most—faith, love, integrity, service, courage, joy. Circle the top three. That's your north star.

- **Face the Fear.**

    List the doubts that nip at your heels. Be blunt. Then write this line under them like a headline: *"God is greater than my limitation."* Cross out every fear once you've written it. (Yes, physically. Drama encouraged.)

- **Take the Next Faithful Step.**

    Legacy starts now, not "someday." Choose one action for the next 24 hours—serve someone quietly, share your faith naturally, encourage a weary friend, reconcile where possible, give generously. Put it on your calendar. Do it.

- **Thread God into the Ordinary.**

    Where can God meet you in your daily rhythms—commute, kitchen, meetings, inbox? Pick one moment you'll repurpose into a sacred habit: a quick prayer before you open your email, a blessing over your family's shoes by the door, Scripture on a sticky note where you most stress-scroll.

- **Rely, Don't Wrestle.**

    Write a one-sentence prayer of dependence: *"Lord, empower me to live beyond my limits today."* Say it morning and night for the next seven days. Watch what shifts.

Declarations for the Journey

Speak these out loud. Let your walls hear them.

- **I am seed and sower.** My small yes multiplies.
- **My limits are not the end of the story.** They're the place God starts.
- **I trade perfection for presence.** I show up; God shows off.
- **I live today like someone's tomorrow depends on it.** Because it might.
- **I will leave holy echoes, not just highlights.** Faith over fame, impact over image.

A Simple Prayer

God of Abraham and of this very moment, anchor my heart to Your promises. Make courage my default and obedience my rhythm. Turn my ordinary into overflow, my weakness into witness, and let the ripples of today carry Your goodness into generations in Jesus name. Amen.

PURPOSE AWAITS

Every sunrise hand you a pen. Write with faith. Walk with purpose. Laugh often—joy is a testimony. When the path narrows, keep moving; when the wind howls, sing anyway. Your life, lived in honest dependence on God, is already building something that time can't erode.

Take that first step today. Then take the next. Leave footprints that look like trust, conversations that smell like grace, and a trail of courage no storm can wash away. This is your legacy: bold, beautiful, and gloriously beyond your limitations—echoing into eternity.

CHAPTER 10

A New Beginning Beyond Limitation

Your Limitations Do Not Define You; God's Power and Grace Define You

Let's say it plain: you are not the sum of your scars, your stumbles, or your "not yet." Limits try to narrate your story; God edits the script. His power shows up best where we feel weakest, and His grace is more than enough for every mile still ahead.

You're not boxed in by what happened, what hurt, or what hasn't happened—physically, emotionally, or circumstantially. You are defined by the God who lovingly crafted you, called you, and equips you. You've been packed for purpose. The bags are already loaded with what you need—courage for the first step, grace for the second, strength for the stretch.

"We are God's handiwork, created in Christ Jesus to do good works, which God prepared in advance for us to do." —Ephesians 2:10

You were designed on purpose, for purpose. The assignments are real. The timing is strategic. The Author is trustworthy.

Step Into Your Next: Purpose, Timing, Mindset

Walk in your God-given mandate and purpose.
Purpose isn't a spotlight; it's a steady lamp for your feet. Start where you stand. If it looks small, smile—God loves to move mountains with mustard seeds.

Trust His timing.
You don't need the aerial view to take the next faithful step. Heaven runs on perfect timing—even delays are choreography.

Embrace a limitless mindset.
The enemy says you're too much or not enough. God says you're chosen, anointed, and backed by His Spirit. That settles it. Release the lies. Upgrade your internal language to match Heaven's verdict.

"I can do all things through Christ who gives me strength." —Philippians 4:13
Translation: If God called you to it, Christ will carry you through it.

Declarations to Reset Your Inner Narrative

- I am crafted by God; purpose is in my DNA.
- My weakness is a runway for God's strength.
- I choose obedience over optics, faith over fear.
- I move at God's pace and still arrive on time.
- I will not bow to limits—only to the Lord.

A Prayer for Strength, Guidance, and Holy Courage

Dear Heavenly Father, Thank You that our identity isn't welded to limitation but anchored in Your power and grace. We are Your handiwork—set apart for good works You already prepared.

Strengthen every reader to step boldly into their calling. When our knees shake, steady our hearts. Let Your power be perfected in our weakness, and remind us You are with us—always.

Guide our choices. Teach us to trust Your timing over our timelines. Evict fear, doubt, and insecurity; move Your promises into the master bedroom of our minds.

Empower us to live beyond circumstance and radiate Your hope. Make us living signposts that point to Your goodness. May our lives echo Your glory and leave a faith-filled legacy that outlives us.

We trust Your strength, Your timing, Your perfect plan. In Jesus' name, Amen.

Embrace the New Beginning

Breathe deep. Shoulders back. Today is not a rerun—it's a premiere. You are not limited by your past, your fears, or your present view. You are empowered by the Spirit of God, and He doesn't do ceilings. Walk boldly. Say yes. Expect grace in motion. The road ahead is rich with possibility, and with God beside you, there is nothing you and He cannot do together.

Reflection Exercises: Understanding and Shaping Your Legacy

1) Reflecting on Your Current Legacy
Why this matters: You've already been leaving footprints. Let's see where they lead.

Do this:
- List the people you've influenced—family, friends, coworkers, neighbors.
- Journal your answers:

- What impact have I had on others?
- What values have I passed on?
- What do I want people to remember about my life?
- Where do I want a stronger, more positive impact?

Action Step: Pick one area to strengthen (e.g., family rhythms, community service, spiritual mentorship). Set a concrete 60–90 day goal—*"Serve monthly at ___," "Call my parents weekly," "Meet with a mentee biweekly."* Put it on your calendar.

2) Designing the Legacy, You Want to Leave

Why this matters: Legacy grows where intention goes.

Do this:
- Envision how you want to be remembered—spiritually, emotionally, practically.
- Journal your answers:
  - What spiritual values do I want to impart?
  - How do I want to be remembered by those I love?
  - What stories of my faith do I want future generations to hear?

Action Step: Choose one small "seed action" for the next month—share your testimony with a loved one, start a simple family tradition (gratitude at dinner, Friday blessing), or begin writing your faith journey.

3) Trusting God to Build Your Legacy
Why this matters: We plant and water; God makes it grow.

"One generation commends Your works to another; they tell of Your mighty acts." —Psalm 145:4

Do this:
- Journal your answers:
  - How am I letting God use my life to build a legacy of faith?
  - Where do I need to trust Him more?
  - How can I shift from self-effort to Spirit-led action?

Action Step: Identify one area where you need to trust God more (finances, health, calling, relationships). Pray daily for wisdom and courage. Take one aligned step this week— *have the conversation, send the application, book the appointment, join the team.*

A Simple Rule of Life (Carry This Forward)

- **Morning:** One scripture, one declaration, one small obedience.
- **Midday:** One person to encourage.

- **Evening:** One gratitude, one surrender.

Repeat. That's how legacies get built—one faithful day at a time.

Step On Limitations

Limits can label, but they don't get the naming rights. God does. So, walk like it. Love like it. Lead like it. Your life—anchored in His strength and aimed at His purpose—will outshine every ceiling and outlast every storm. Onward.

CHAPTER 11

Personal Legacy

Leaving a Faith-Filled Legacy

Let's keep it real: trophies gather dust, but a life of faith gathers people. Leaving a legacy isn't just about what's in your will; it's about what's in your walk. It's the values you embody, the beliefs you practice, the stories of God's goodness you keep telling until hope wakes up in someone else. That's legacy—love and truth, lived loud and passed on.

What Is a Legacy of Faith?

A legacy of faith is a living inheritance—God's goodness carried from heart to heart, generation to generation. It's not merely what you leave behind; it's what you pour out along the way. Every step of trust, every yes to Scripture, every act of mercy leaves footprints others can follow. Your children may hold your last name, but your neighbors, coworkers, and community can carry your spiritual DNA.

My Wake-Up Call to Legacy

For years, I was busy—goals, calendars, grind. Then one ordinary day, while I was with my kids, it hit me like a holy lightning bolt: *they're learning how to live by watching me live.* My reactions were discipling them. My habits were shaping their hope. So, I got intentional.

We opened the Bible together—messy, honest, consistent. I told them stories of God's faithfulness from our family history and from Scripture. We practiced integrity in the small things and service in the unseen places. Nothing fancy—just steady. That's when I realized: legacy is built in the daily, and the daily is where God does His best work. My prayer now? That my children—and anyone who crosses my path—will catch courage from my life, trust God's promises, and love people big.

Three Biblical Blueprints for Legacy

1) Abraham — Legacy of Faith

God's promise was clear: **"I will make you into a great nation... and you will be a blessing"** (Genesis 12:2–3). Abraham said yes without a map, and his faith didn't end with him—it multiplied through Isaac, Jacob, and the people of Israel.

Lesson: Faith is generational. Your obedience today becomes someone else's momentum tomorrow.

2) David — Legacy of Worship and Obedience
Before David died, he charged Solomon: **"Be strong… walk in obedience to the Lord"** (1 Kings 2:2–3). David's life—repentant, worshipful, wholehearted—set Solomon up to build the temple.

Lesson: Your relationship with God sets the spiritual temperature of your house. Live it hot.

3) Timothy — Legacy of Spiritual Mentorship
Paul saw the faith that lived first in Timothy's grandmother Lois and mother Eunice (2 Timothy 1:5). Mentorship and family discipleship braided together to raise a world-changer.

Lesson: Legacy grows through relationships. Teach, model, encourage—repeat.

How to Build Your Legacy of Faith (Starting Now)
- **Clarify your core.**
  Name the top three values you want people to feel when they're around you—faith, integrity, generosity, courage, joy, service. Circle them. Own them.

- **Make it visible.**
  Let your faith show up in habits: prayer before you open your inbox; Scripture on your mirror; gratitude at dinner; forgiveness on speed dial.

- **Tell the stories.**
  Share testimonies of God's faithfulness—how He provided, healed, guided. Your stories are scaffolding for someone else's trust.

- **Disciple in the daily.**
  Invite your kids, friends, mentees into ordinary obedience—serving a neighbor, giving generously, apologizing quickly, worshiping wholeheartedly.

- **Choose consistency over perfection.**
  Legacy is a long game. Miss a day? Get back up. Small seeds. Steady rain. Big harvest.

Declarations for the Journey

- I am planting what I want to see multiplied.
- My small yes today becomes a great blessing tomorrow.
- I don't pass down fear; I pass down faith.
- My house will be a lighthouse—worshiping, serving, obeying.
- God's goodness in me will outlive me.

Quick Legacy Action Plan

- **This Week:** Share one faith story with a child, friend, or mentee.
- **This Month:** Start a simple tradition (family prayer, Sunday service project, Scripture memory).
- **Next 90 Days:** Mentor one person intentionally—meet biweekly, pray together, set spiritual goals.
- **Ongoing:** Track "God-sightings" in a journal; read them aloud at the end of each month.

The Mirror of Legacy

Legacy is less about monuments and more about mirrors—lives that reflect God's love and truth. So, walk it out with joy. Let your faith be loud enough to echo and gentle enough to heal. Build what lasts. And remember: you're not just leaving something behind—you're launching someone forward.

CONCLUSION: *The Echo You Leave*

Let's land this plane with the truth pulsing through every chapter: you are not a footnote—you are a living letter from God, written in grace and addressed to the world. Limits may try to narrate your story, but they don't own the pen. Faith does. Love does. The God who called you most certainly does.

You've gathered tools—purpose, obedience, courage, consistency. You've practiced the holy art of small steps. You've seen how legacy isn't marble and monuments; it's fingerprints on hearts, ripples on water, light passed hand to hand like a candle that refuses to go out.

Here's the charge:

- ✓ **Walk it out.** Start where your feet are. Let your everyday become the altar where trust is offered and joy is kindled.
- ✓ **Speak it out.** Tell the stories of God's goodness until hope wakes up in someone else's eyes.
- ✓ **Live it out.** Choose presence over perfection, obedience over optics, devotion over distraction.

Your Legacy Manifesto

- ✓ I will plant what I want multiplied—faith, kindness, courage, truth.
- ✓ I will trade hurry for holiness and performance for presence.
- ✓ I will let God's strength run through my weakness and call it beautiful.
- ✓ I will leave holy echoes, not just highlights.
- ✓ I will live today like someone's tomorrow depends on it—because it might.

A Simple Rule for the Road

- ✓ **Daily:** One scripture, one declaration, one act of love.
- ✓ **Weekly:** One intentional conversation, one quiet hour with God, one generous yes.
- ✓ **Monthly:** One testimony shared, one habit reviewed, one step into something that scares you (in the best way).

A Prayer to Carry

Lord, write Your courage across my days. Turn my small yes into wide-open ripple. Make my ordinary a lighthouse, my weakness a witness, and my life a road sign to Your goodness. Lead me—then use me—so future generations find You faithful in Jesus name. Amen.

JOURNAL SECTION

Welcome Phenomenal One

Welcome to the journal section—your launchpad from inspiration to action. Over the next 45 days, these guided prompts will help you clear the fog, confront limiting beliefs, and turn small, faithful steps into holy momentum. Each entry pairs soul-deep reflection with a simple, doable action so you don't just *feel* motivated—you actually move. Use this space to capture God-sightings, craft declarations that steady your heart, and design rhythms that keep you lit from the inside out. Bring your honest thoughts, your brave questions, and your expectant hope. This is where your legacy stops being an idea and starts becoming your daily life.

Journal Notes

Days 1–15: Identity & Courage

God's Letter, Not a Footnote — Where has God rewritten your story lately? *(2 Cor. 3:3)*
Action: Write one-sentence identity statement.

Journal Notes

Strength in the Soft Spots — Which weakness is becoming a witness? *(2 Cor. 12:9)*
Action: List one way to lean into grace today.

Journal Notes

Holy Small Steps — What's one "mustard seed" move you'll take? *(Matt. 17:20)*
Action: Put it on your calendar.

Journal Notes

Fear's Last Stand — Name the fear; answer it with truth. *(Ps. 56:3–4)*
Action: Speak a 10-word declaration aloud.

Journal Notes

Joy on Ordinary Streets — Where did joy sparkle in your routine? *(Neh. 8:10)*
Action: Schedule a 10-minute joy break tomorrow.

Journal Notes

Presence over Perfection — What will you do imperfectly but faithfully? *(Luke 10:41–42)*
Action: Set a timer and start.

Journal Notes

Obedience in Motion — When did you choose God's "yes" over your comfort? *(John 14:15)* **Action:** Text one person your obedience win.

Journal Notes

Holy Confidence — What evidence says "you can't," and what promise says "with God, you can"? *(Phil. 4:13)*
Action: Post the promise where you'll see it.

Journal Notes

Knees Knocking, Heart Steady — Recall a moment you acted brave while afraid. *(Josh. 1:9)*
Action: Plan the next brave step.

Journal Notes

Voice of Testimony — Tell a mini-story of God's goodness in 5 lines. *(Ps. 9:1)*
Action: Share it with one person.

Journal Notes

Trading Hurry for Holy — Where will you slow down to listen? *(Ps. 46:10)*
Action: 5 silent minutes today.

Journal Notes

Sacred Boundaries — What do you need to say "no" to protect your "yes"? *(Prov. 4:23)*
Action: Write and send one boundary message.

Journal Notes

Gratitude as Warfare — List 10 thank-You that defy your mood. *(1 Thess. 5:18)*
Action: Send one thank-you note.

Journal Notes

Renewed Mindset — Replace one limiting belief with heaven's language. *(Rom. 12:2)*
Action: Repeat the new belief 3x today.

Journal Notes

Anointed Assignment — Name your current assignment and why it matters. *(Eph. 2:10)*
Action: Outline next three micro-steps.

Journal Notes

Days 16–30: Relationships & Legacy

Holy Echoes — Who echoes in your life? Honor them. *(Heb. 13:7)*
Action: Write them a tribute.

Journal Notes

A House that Worships — What rhythms tune your home to God? *(Ps. 34:3)*
Action: Add one simple ritual.

Journal Notes

Mentor & Be Mentored — Who needs your hand? Who holds yours? *(2 Tim. 1:5–6)*
Action: Book both conversations.

Journal Notes

Forgiveness that Frees — Who do you need to release? *(Matt. 6:14–15)*
Action: Pray their name with blessing.

Journal Notes

Table Ministry — Who belongs at your table this month? *(Rom. 12:13)*
Action: Send an invite.

Journal Notes

Words that Build — Audit your speech: where can you add life? *(Prov. 18:21)*
Action: Send a voice memo of encouragement.

Journal Notes

Generosity Flow — Where can you give time, treasure, or talent? *(2 Cor. 9:7–8)*
Action: Give one meaningful gift.

Journal Notes

Reconcilers Walk First — What step toward peace can you initiate? *(Matt. 5:23–24)*
Action: Draft the first message.

Journal Notes

Parenting / Influence with Purpose — What do you want the next generation to *feel* from you? *(Ps. 78:4)*
Action: Plan a shared faith moment.

Journal Notes

Servant Leadership — How do you lead like Jesus where you are? *(Mark 10:45)*
Action: Do an unseen act of service.

Journal Notes

Legacy Stories — Capture a family God-story before it's lost. *(Deut. 6:6–9)*
Action: Record a 3-minute audio story.

Journal Notes

Community Roots — Where will you plant deeper locally? *(Jer. 29:7)*
Action: Join or volunteer once.

Journal Notes

Blessing Your Workplace — Pray over your work and coworkers. *(Col. 3:23)*
Action: Write a workplace blessing.

Journal Notes

Conflict with Kindness — How will you disagree with grace? *(Eph. 4:2–3)*
Action: Script one gracious phrase.

Journal Notes

Passing the Torch — Who are you actively equipping? *(2 Tim. 2:2)*
Action: Share one resource.

Journal Notes

Days 31–45: Purpose, Habits & Holy Momentum

Rule of Life Refresh — What daily/weekly rhythms still serve you? *(Ps. 90:12)*
Action: Keep one, tweak one, drop one.

Angela Gadiare

Journal Notes

Sacred Morning — Design a start you'll actually keep. *(Mark 1:35)*
Action: Set tomorrow's cue (place Bible, mug, pen).

Journal Notes

Courage Calendar — Book one "faith stretch" this month. *(Isa. 54:2)*
Action: Put it on the calendar.

Journal Notes

Steward the Body — How will you honor God with your health? *(1 Cor. 6:19–20)*
Action: One nourishing choice today.

Journal Notes

Financial Faithfulness — What's your next wise step with money? *(Prov. 3:9–10)*
Action: Automate a give/save move.

Journal Notes

Creative Offering — What can you make with God this week? *(Ex. 35:35)*
Action: Schedule a creation session.

I Am Beyond Limitations

Journal Notes

Wilderness Wisdom — Which desert taught you most? *(Deut. 8:2)*
Action: List the gifts you carried out.

Journal Notes

Open Doors & Closed Ones — Which shut door saved you? *(Rev. 3:7–8)*
Action: Thank God for the no.

Journal Notes

Holy Rest — What does true Sabbath look like for you? *(Matt. 11:28–29)*
Action: Block 2–4 hours of rest.

Journal Notes

Spiritual Authority — Where do you need to speak life boldly? *(Luke 10:19)*
Action: Pray scripture over that space.

I Am Beyond Limitations

Journal Notes

Prophetic Imagination — Write a scene from the future you're building with God. *(Hab. 2:2–3)*
Action: Read it aloud.

Journal Notes

Audit the Echo — If someone shadowed you today, what legacy would they feel? *(Phil. 4:9)*
Action: Change one habit tomorrow.

Journal Notes

Testimony Trail — Log three fresh God-sightings this week. *(Ps. 105:1–2)*
Action: Share one publicly.

Journal Notes

Finish Lines & New Starts — Where is God saying "well done," and where is He saying "begin"? *(Isa. 43:19)*
Action: Celebrate one win; start one new thing.

Journal Notes

Blessing Release — Write a blessing you'll pray over your people for the next 30 days. *(Num. 6:24–26)*
Action: Pray it today—and tomorrow.

A Final Blessing

May your heart stay soft and your spine stay strong. May your table be long and your memory short—especially for offenses. May you laugh often, forgive quickly, and obey promptly. May your ceilings become someone else's floors, and may your last word always be love.

Close this book, but don't you dare close your heart. There's a world waiting for your light. Step forward with joy. Walk boldly in your God-given purpose. Leave a legacy that sounds like freedom and shines like.

www.ingramcontent.com/pod-product-compliance
Lightning Source LLC
Chambersburg PA
CBHW050644160426
43194CB00010B/1797